THE MICROWAVE LIBRARY

COOKING WITH

Fish

ELIZABETH CORNISH

D1511965

THE MICROWAVE LIBRARY

COOKING WITH

Fish

ELIZABETH CORNISH

GALLERY BOOKS

An Imprint of W. H. Smith Publishers Inc.
112 Madison Avenue
New York City 10016

THE
MICROWAVE
LIBRARY

A QUINTET BOOK
produced for
GALLERY BOOKS
An imprint of W.H. Smith Publishers Inc.
112 Madison Avenue,
New York, New York 10016

ISBN 0 8317 5971 2

This book was designed and produced by
Quintet Publishing Limited
6 Blundell Street London N7

Art Director: Peter Bridgewater
Photographers: Michael Bull and Trevor Wood
Home Economist: Veronica Bull

Typeset in Great Britain by
Central Southern Typesetters, Eastbourne
Manufactured in Hong Kong by
Regent Publishing Services Limited
Printed in Hong Kong by
Leefung-Asco Printers Limited

CONTENTS

FISH

ANYONE who has ever tasted
fish cooked in a microwave
will agree that there is no better way
of retaining its succulence,
freshness, delicacy of flavour and
fineness of texture.

Fish is so moist that it can be
cooked in little or no liquid or fat, so
none of its flavour is lost or changed.
It can also be cooked very fast, so it
won't go dry or rubbery.

Fish is an excellent source of
protein, vitamins and minerals and is
becoming increasingly popular,
particularly in comparison with
meat, because it is less fat.

As people eat more and more fish,
so the selection available grows and
unusual varieties begin to appear.
There are at least 50 types of edible
fish, so most of us have many more to
look forward to.

This book features a large
selection of fish, among them cod,
plaice, herring, monkfish, snapper
and mullet and many others, all
types of seafood and molluscs, and
even eel and squid. If you find a fish
that you haven't tried before which
isn't in the book, ask for advice on its
preparation when you buy it. You
will certainly be able to adapt several
recipes to suit different fish because
most of them, soft- or firm-fleshed
are cooked in the same way.

Perhaps in the past the plainness
of traditional fish cooking has put
some people off eating it more than
once a week. It's just as easy to be
adventurous with fish as with any
other food, you can that looks create
something spectacular and tastes
exciting with very little effort.

Fish is such a clean and simple
food and it lends itself perfectly to
dishes that are bright and elegant
with combinations of tastes that
surprise and delight. As these dishes
take such little time to prepare,
you   will be able to cook
for a dinner party every night of
the week.

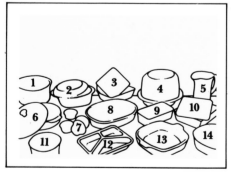

A selection of cookware, some of it specially designed for the microwave oven, which is suitable for microwaving.

1 Thorpak cake dish 2 Thorpak casserole dish
3 Microware freezer dishes 4 Roasting dish
5 Thorpak jug 6 Browning dish 7 Minidishes
(ramekins) 8 Double microwave serving dish
9 Glass loaf pan 10 Glass casserole with lid
11 Cake or soufflé dish 12 Three-section
vegetable dish 13 Browning dish 14 Glass
ovenproof dish

ABOUT THE MICROWAVE OVEN

IF YOU are new to cooking with the microwave, the first thing to do is to read the instruction booklet supplied with your model. This will tell you all you need to know about how your cooker works and how to operate it.

Microwave cookers work by emitting concentrated infra red radiation that penetrates and therefore heats food much faster than conventional cookers. They consequently save considerably on cooking time.

The microwave is like any other kitchen appliance that makes life easier for the cook. Once you are used to it, which takes remarkably little time for such a sophisticated gadget, experience will tell you how long it will take to cook or reheat a given dish. If in doubt, always undercook – you can easily add on another minute or so.

To familiarize yourself with the cooker try baking a potato. Scrub the potato and prick the skin a few times with a fork. Lay it on a piece of absorbent kitchen paper and cook on full power for about 6 minutes for a 175 g/6 oz potato. Stop cooking half-way through to turn the potato over. A successfully baked potato will demonstrate how easy microwave cooking is.

Remember to stir or rearrange items during cooking or the food may not be evenly cooked, and

always cover a dish with a lid or cling film (plastic wrap) which you have pierced in two or three places with a knife to make vents through which the steam can escape.

Don't use anything metallic in the microwave, and this includes china decorated with silver or gold leaf. If you want to test if a dish is microwave-proof, put it in the oven next to a cup of water and cook on full for a minute. If the water is hot and the dish stays cool, it is safe to use. If the dish is hotter than the water, avoid using it.

Always prick the skins of vegetables and fish to prevent them from bursting. Eggs should always be pricked for the same reason. Never put an egg in its shell in the microwave – it will explode.

Where the recipe times in this book are not specific, this is to avoid errors. A microwave may be a scientific instrument, but neither cooks nor food can be standardized. No two carrots are the same shape and no two cooks cut them up in the same way. It is *always* safer to undercook and test.

Crockery, cutlery (flatware, glassware and cookware such as this must NOT be used in a microwave oven.

1 Ceramics with metal decoration **2** Dishes with metal decoration and glazes containing metal **3** Cutlery (silverware or flatware) **4** Metal flan tin and disposable foil bakeware **5** Glassware with metal rim or bands **6** Metal pots and pans **7** Metal bakeware **8** Metal skewers or fondue forks

PAELLA

SERVES 4 / SET: FULL

Ingredients

15 ml/1 tbsp olive oil
1 onion, finely sliced
1 clove garlic, crushed (minced)
1 good cup/250 g/8 oz long-grain rice
a few strands of saffron
2½ cups/600 ml/1 pt boiling chicken stock
salt and freshly ground black pepper
1¾ cups/200 g/7 oz peas
1 generous cup/175 g/6 oz peeled prawns, (shrimp) plus a few in their shells for garnish
⅔ cup/100 g/4 oz cooked chicken, chopped
⅔ cup/100 g/4 oz cooked ham, chopped
5 cups/600 ml/1 pt mussels, scrubbed and rinsed
2½ cups/300 ml/½ pt clams, thoroughly rinsed
small glass of dry white wine

It is important to scrub the mussels
thoroughly under running water to remove
their beards and any grit. Discard any
shells that are open or broken.

◆ Put the oil in a large pot and cook
for 30 seconds. Stir in the onion and
garlic and cook for 2 minutes. Stir in
the rice and saffron, pour over the
boiling stock, add seasoning, cover
and cook for 8 minutes.

◆ Stir in the peas, prawns (shrimp),
chicken and ham, cover and cook for
4 minutes. Leave the pot to stand,
covered, while you cook the mussels
and clams.

◆ Put the mussels and clams in a
large pot and pour over the wine.
Cook for about 3 minutes, until the
shells have opened. Discard any shells
that remain closed.

◆ Arrange the paella on a heated
serving plate. Take some of the
mussels and clams out of their shells
and add to the rice. Garnish the dish
with the remaining mussels, clams and
prawns (shrimp).

VARIATION Add scallops and pieces of
cooked pork.

SALMON STEAKS WITH HOLLANDAISE SAUCE

SERVES 4 / SET: DEFROST AND FULL

Ingredients

½ cup/100 g/4 oz butter, diced
30 ml/2 tbsp lemon juice
3 egg yolks
salt and white pepper
4 salmon steaks, about 175 g/6 oz each

Serve this dish on a special occasion with new peas and new potatoes. Salmon is so succulent that it will cook perfectly without the addition of any water or fat.

◆ First make the sauce. Put the butter in a bowl and cook for 2 minutes on medium or defrost until melted. Add the lemon juice and the egg yolks and whisk lightly.

◆ Cook on medium or defrost for 1 minute, whisk again and season with salt and white pepper (black pepper would spoil the appearance of the sauce). Transfer the sauce to a heated jug and keep warm while you cook the salmon.

◆ Rinse the salmon steaks, pat dry and lay in a shallow dish. Cover with vented cling wrap (plastic wrap) and cook on full for 3½–4 minutes, turning the dish once.

◆ Serve the salmon steaks with the Hollandaise sauce.

◆ This dish is equally good served cold, but not chilled.

FISHERMAN'S PIE

SERVES 4 / SET: FULL

Ingredients

750 g/1½ lb smoked cod or haddock fillets, skinned

1¼ cups/100 g/4 oz mushrooms

4 small leeks, sliced

1¼ cups/300 ml/½ pt milk

3 tbsp/40 g/1½ oz butter

6 tbsp/40 g/1½ oz flour

6 tbsp/40 g/1½ oz Gruyère cheese, grated

4½ tbsp/40 g/1½ oz Parmesan cheese, grated

salt and freshly ground black pepper

2 hardboiled (hard-cooked) eggs, sliced

1½ cups/250 g/8 oz prawns (shrimp), peeled

3 cups/750 g/1½ lb potatoes, cooked and mashed with plenty of butter and a little milk

◆ Put the fish fillets in a deep pie dish with the mushrooms and leeks and add about 60 ml/4 tbsp of the milk. Cover and cook for 3–4 minutes until fish is tender. Pour off the milk and reserve. Flake the fish with a fork.
◆ Put the butter in a jug or bowl and cook for 1 minute, until melted. Stir in the flour. Cook for 1 minute. Pour on the milk the fish was cooked in and the remaining milk. Cook for 3 minutes, whisking the sauce after each minute. Add the cheeses and season. Cook for a further minute and whisk again.
◆ Combine the fish, mushrooms, leeks, eggs and prawns (shrimp) in the pie dish and stir in the sauce. Top with the mashed potato and heat through for about 4 minutes.
◆ Brown the top under the grill (broiler) if liked before serving.

Fisherman's pie

FRIED COD'S ROE

SERVES 1 / SET: FULL

Ingredients

a little flour

1 cod's roe

a little beaten egg

1 cup/50 g/2 oz fresh breadcrumbs (approx.)

1 tbsp/15 g/½ oz butter

lemon wedges

The cod's roe that you buy will have already been cooked. Fried cod's roe makes a very nourishing lunch for one with a crisp salad.

◆ Sprinkle flour over the roe to coat it evenly. Dust off the excess. Roll it in egg, then in breadcrumbs, pushing them on with your fingers.
◆ Heat a browning dish to maximum according to the manufacturer's instructions. Put the butter on the dish and, wearing oven gloves, tilt it so that it is covered in hot fat.
◆ Put the roe on the dish and cook for 30–45 seconds on each side.
◆ Let it stand for 1 minute, then serve with lemon wedges.

HOMEMADE FISH CAKES IN TOMATO SAUCE

SERVES 4–6 / SET: FULL

Ingredients

500 g/1 lb cod, skin and bones removed
45 ml/3 tbsp water
500 g/1 lb even size potatoes
3 tbsp/40 g/1½ oz butter
6 tbsp/40 g/1½ oz flour
1¼ cups/300 ml/½ pt milk
chopped parsley
salt and freshly ground black pepper
golden breadcrumbs
TOMATO SAUCE
15 ml/1 tbsp oil
1 onion, chopped
1 clove garlic, crushed (minced)
1½ cups/400 g/14 oz tinned (canned) tomatoes, drained
15 ml/1 tbsp tomato purée (paste)

◆ Put the cod in a dish with the water. Cover with vented cling wrap (plastic wrap) and cook for 4 minutes, until done. Drain and flake the cod with a fork.

◆ Put the potatoes in the oven and cook for 4–7 minutes, depending on their size, rearranging once. When they are done, remove and allow them to cool. Remove the skins and mash the potato well.

◆ Put the butter in a bowl and cook for 1 minute. Stir in the flour and cook for 1 minute. Stir in the milk and cook for 3 minutes, whisking after each minute.

◆ Mix the fish and potatoes together and bind with the sauce. Add enough sauce so that you have a very stiff mixture. Mix in the parsley and seasoning.

◆ Form the mixture into cakes. Roll them in golden breadcrumbs and set aside while you make the tomato sauce.

◆ Put the oil in a bowl and mix in the onion and garlic. Cook for 2 minutes. Add the tomatoes, tomato purée (paste) and seasoning. Cook for 3 minutes. Mix until smooth in the liquidizer. Return to the oven to heat through for 2 minutes.

◆ Cook the fish cakes. Heat a browning dish to maximum, according to the manufacturer's instructions, and cook the cakes in batches of 3 for 3 minutes each, turning them over half-way through. If you have no browning dish, they can be cooked on a greased plate, but they won't be crisp.

◆ Spoon a pool of sauce onto each plate and lay the fish cakes in it. Serve at once.

VARIATION This is an excellent way of serving bought fish fingers (fish sticks).

FILLETS OF PLAICE (FLOUNDER) WITH GRAPES, ALMONDS AND SCAMPI

SERVES 4 / SET: FULL

Ingredients

12 large green grapes

75 g/3 oz toasted flaked (slivered) almonds

8 scampi

²/₃ cup/150 ml/¼ pt tinned (canned) consommé

15 ml/1 tbsp sherry

4 plaice (flounder) fillets, skinned

a little butter

◆ Halve the grapes and remove the pips (seeds). Put them in a dish with the flaked (slivered) almonds, scampi, consommé and sherry and cook for 2–3 minutes, until hot through. Keep warm.

◆ Lay the plaice (flounder) fillets in a buttered dish and dot with butter. Cover with vented cling wrap (plastic wrap) and cook for 2–3 minutes, turning once, until cooked through.

◆ Put the fillets on 4 heated plates and spoon the sauce around them. Serve at once.

Fillets of plaice (flounder) with grapes, almonds and scampi

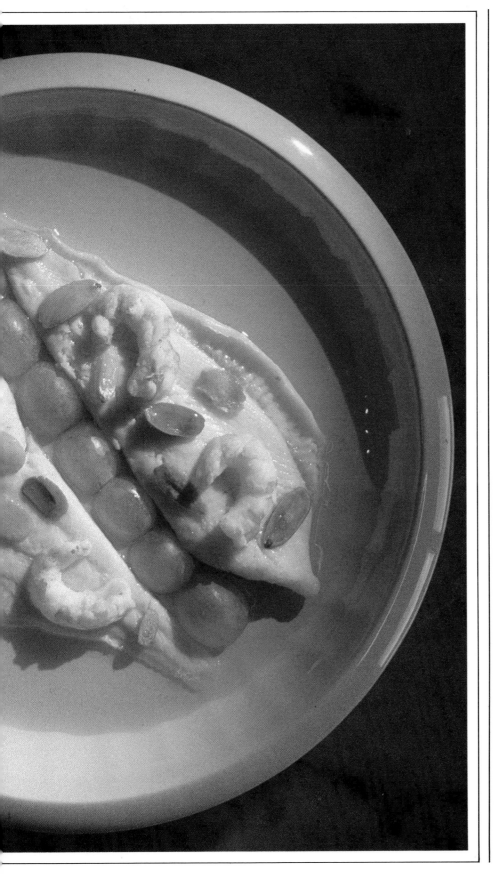

FISH IN VERMOUTH SAUCE

SERVES 4 / SET: FULL

Ingredients

15 ml/1 tbsp oil

1 shallot, chopped

1 cup/75 g/3 oz mushrooms, wiped and sliced

30 ml/2 tbsp dry vermouth

2/3 cup/150 ml/1/4 pt single (light) cream

salt

cayenne pepper

4 fillets white fish

a little butter

Use any white fish fillets for this recipe.

◆ First make the sauce. Put the oil in a dish and cook for 30 seconds. Add the shallot and cook for 2 minutes. Add the mushrooms and vermouth, cover with vented cling wrap (plastic wrap) and cook for 3 minutes, stirring once.

◆ Stir in the cream and season to taste with salt and cayenne pepper. Set aside.

◆ Put the fish fillets in a dish and dot with butter. Cover with vented cling wrap (plastic wrap) and cook for 3–4 minutes, until done, rearranging once.

◆ Heat the sauce through for 1 minute

◆ Lay the fish fillets on heated plates, pour over the sauce and serve.

HADDOCK IN SWEET AND SOUR SAUCE

SERVES 2—4 / SET: FULL

Ingredients

15 ml/1 tbsp minced onion
1 clove garlic, crushed (minced)
2 hot chillies (chilis), seeded and finely sliced
1 slice ginger, grated
45 ml/3 tbsp sherry
4 haddock fillets, weighing about 500 g/1 lb in total
¾ cup/200 g/7 oz tinned (canned) tomatoes, drained and sieved (strained)
15 ml/1 tbsp tomato purée (paste)
a pinch of sugar
finely shredded spring onions (scallions)
tomato slices

Serve this dish with fluffy white rice.

◆ For the marinade, mix together in a dish the onion, garlic, chillies (chilis), ginger and sherry. Lay the fish in the marinade and leave for an hour, turning occasionally.

◆ Mix together the tomatoes, tomato purée (paste) and sugar and pour over the fish. Cover with vented cling wrap (plastic wrap) and cook for about 5 minutes, until done, turning once.

◆ Serve garnished with finely shredded spring onions (scallions) and tomato slices.

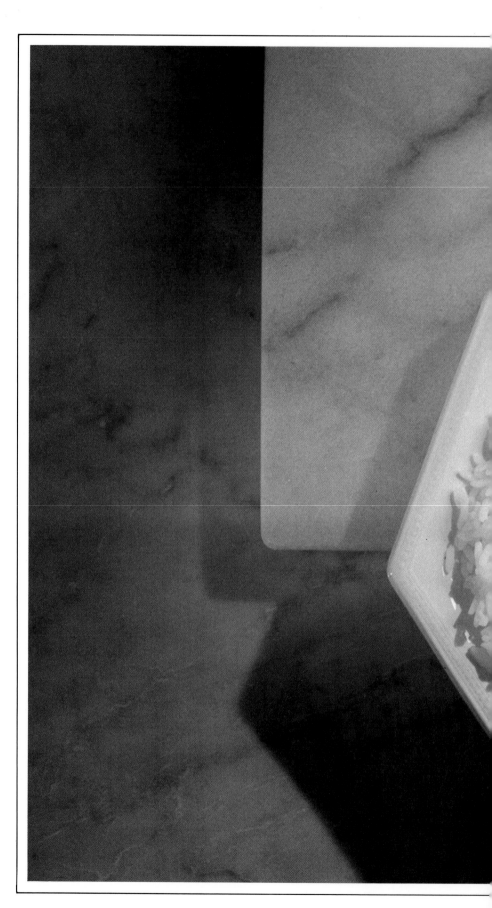

FILLETS OF MACKEREL WITH CRANBERRY SAUCE

SERVES 4 / SET: FULL

Ingredients
2 large mackerel
2 cups/250 g/8 oz cranberries
30 ml/2 tbsp lemon juice
15 ml/1 tbsp port
salt and freshly ground black pepper
radicchio

A colourful and tasty winter dish.

◆ Fillet the fish. Gut the mackerel, cut off the fins and carefully remove the bone from the head downwards. Cut off the heads. Remove the skin and the remaining bones.
◆ Make the sauce. Combine the cranberries, lemon juice and port in a bowl and season with salt and pepper. Cook for 4 minutes, until the berries are soft. Keep warm.
◆ Lay the fish in a shallow dish, cover with vented cling wrap (plastic wrap) and cook for 4 minutes, turning once.
◆ Arrange the mackerel fillets on heated plates, on a bed of radicchio, pour over the sauce and serve.

VARIATION Try using gooseberries instead of cranberries.

FILLETS OF COD WITH CAPER SAUCE

S E R V E S   4   /   S E T :   F U L L

Ingredients

3 tbsp/40 g/1½ oz butter
6 tbsp/40 g/1½ oz flour
1¼ cups/300 ml/½ pt milk
30 ml/2 tbsp capers, chopped
10 ml/2 tsp vinegar from the caper jar
salt and pepper
4 cod fillets
a little butter

◆ First make the sauce. Put the butter in a bowl and cook for 45 seconds. Stir in the flour. Pour on the milk and cook for 3 minutes, whisking after each minute. Stir in the capers and vinegar and season to taste with salt and pepper.

◆ Put the cod fillets in a dish and dot with butter. Cover with vented cling wrap (plastic wrap) and cook for 3–4 minutes, turning once.

◆ Put the cod on heated plates, pour over the sauce and serve.

TROUT WITH CUCUMBER AND MUSHROOM

S E R V E S   4   /   S E T :   F U L L   A N D   M E D I U M

Ingredients

¼ cucumber, sliced
2 cups/100 g/4 oz mushrooms, sliced
⅔ cup/150 ml/¼ pt tinned (canned) consommé
4 small trout of even size
60 ml/4 tbsp water
parsley
lemon wedges

◆ Put the cucumber and mushrooms in a dish and pour over the consommé. Cover with vented cling wrap (plastic wrap) and cook for 4 minutes. Set aside.

◆ Put the trout in a dish, add the water, cover with vented cling wrap (plastic wrap) and cook for 4 minutes, turning once, until cooked through.

◆ Put the trout on heated plates and pour the sauce over.

◆ Serve garnished with parsley and lemon wedges.

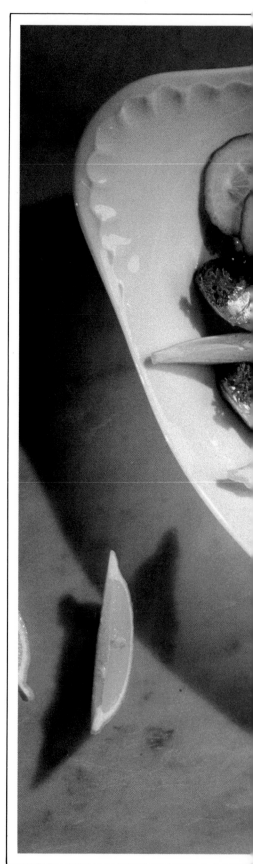

Trout with cucumber and mushroom

MACKEREL WITH ORANGE

SERVES 4 / SET: FULL

Ingredients

4 even-sized mackerel, gutted
grated rind of 1 orange
juice of 2 oranges
2 sprigs rosemary (optional)
1/3 cup/50 g/2 oz black olives, stoned (pitted)
salt and freshly ground black pepper
thin orange slices
curly endive

The tartness of the orange and the blandness of the rice counteract the oiliness of the fish.

◆ Make several slanting slashes with a sharp knife across both sides of each fish to stop the skins bursting, and lay them in a shallow dish. Sprinkle on the orange rind, pour over the juice, add the rosemary (if used) and olives and marinate for 2 hours, turning occasionally.

◆ Baste the fish and cover with vented cling wrap (plastic wrap). Cook for 2–3 minutes.

◆ Turn the fish over, baste and return to the oven, giving the dish a half turn. Cook for a further 2–3 minutes, depending on the size of the fish. Test by inserting the point of a sharp knife as far as the backbone. If the flesh is white and will come away readily, the fish is cooked.

◆ Spoon the marinade over the fish, season and garnish with orange slices and curly endive.

◆ Serve with rice.

FISH WITH FENNEL SAUCE

SERVES 4 / SET: FULL

Ingredients

1/2 fennel bulb, chopped
30 ml/2 tbsp water
3 tbsp/40 g/1 1/2 oz butter
6 tbsp/40 g/1 1/2 oz flour
1 1/4 cups/300 ml/1/2 pt milk
salt and pepper
4 fillets white fish
a little butter
chopped fennel leaves

Fennel goes particularly well with fish – use any white fish in this recipe.

◆ First make the sauce. Put the fennel in a dish with the water. Cover with vented cling wrap (plastic wrap) and cook for 5 minutes, until tender, stirring once. Set aside.

◆ Put the butter in a bowl and cook for 30 seconds. Stir in the flour. Pour on the milk and cook for 3 minutes, whisking after each minute. Stir in the fennel and season with salt and pepper. Keep warm.

◆ Cook the fish. Put the fillets in a dish and dot with butter. Cover with vented cling wrap (plastic wrap) and cook for 3–4 minutes until done.

◆ Lay the fillets on heated plates, pour the sauce over and garnish with chopped fennel leaves.

VARIATION You can make an onion sauce in the same way.

Mackerel with orange

FILLETS OF PLAICE (FLOUNDER) IN PARSLEY SAUCE

SERVES 4 / SET: FULL

Ingredients

3 tbsp/40 g/1½ oz butter

6 tbsp/40 g/1½ oz flour

1¼ cups/300 ml/½ pt milk

salt and freshly ground black pepper

60 ml/4 tbsp finely chopped parsley

4 plaice (flounder) fillets

30 ml/2 tbsp lemon juice

parsley sprigs

lemon wedges

◆ First make the sauce. Put the butter in a bowl and cook for 30 seconds. Stir in the flour. Pour on the milk and cook for 3 minutes, whisking after each minute. Season with salt and pepper and stir in the parsley.

◆ Lay the fish in a dish and dot with butter. Add the lemon juice and cover with vented cling wrap (plastic wrap). Cook for 3–4 minutes, until done, turning the dish once.

◆ Heat the sauce through for 1 minute.

◆ Lay the fish on 4 heated plates, pour over the sauce and garnish with parsley sprigs.

◆ Serve with lemon wedges.

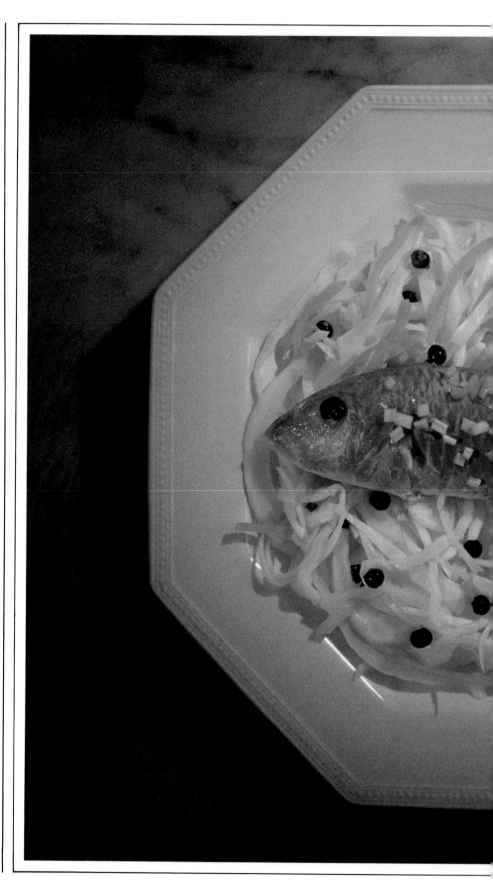

RED MULLET ON A BED OF SHREDDED VEGETABLES

SERVES 4 / SET: FULL

Ingredients

4 red mullet, about 175 g/6 oz each, scaled and gutted

juice of 1 lemon

30 ml/2 tbsp water

approx. 2 cups/250 g/8 oz carrots, finely shredded

approx. 3 cups/250 g/8 oz white cabbage, finely shredded

15 ml/1 tbsp juniper berries

15 ml/1 tbsp clear honey

snipped chives

◆ Put the mullet in a dish with 15 ml/ 1 tbsp of the lemon juice mixed with the water. Cover with vented cling wrap (plastic wrap) and cook for 4 minutes, turning once, until done. Keep warm.

◆ Mix together the carrots, cabbage and juniper berries in a bowl. Pour over the remaining lemon juice mixed with the honey and toss well. Cover with vented cling wrap (plastic wrap) and cook for about 3 minutes, until the vegetables are tender but not too soft.

◆ Arrange the vegetables on 4 heated serving plates and lay the mullet on top.

◆ Garnish with snipped chives and serve at once.

Red mullet on a bed of shredded vegetables

HADDOCK AND VEGETABLES ON A BED OF NOODLES

S E R V E S   4 / S E T :   F U L L

Ingredients

3 tbsp/40 g/1½ oz butter
6 tbsp/40 g/1½ oz flour
⅔ cup/150 ml/¼ pt milk
⅔ cup/150 ml/¼ pt single (light) cream
4½ tbsp/40 g/1½ oz Parmesan cheese
1 egg yolk
4 haddock fillets, about 175 g/6 oz each, skinned
30–45 ml/2–3 tbsp milk
1¾ cups/200 g/7 oz asparagus spears
1 cup/200 g/7 oz broad (fava) beans, cooked or canned
250 g/8 oz fresh spinach tagliatelle
boiling water
salt
5 ml/1 tsp oil
paprika

◆ First make the sauce. Put the butter in a bowl and cook for 1 minute. Stir in the flour and cook for 1 minute. Stir in the milk and cook for 2 minutes, whisking after each minute. Stir in the cream and cheese and cook for 2 minutes, whisking after each minute. Stir in the egg yolk. Keep the sauce warm.

◆ Put the haddock in a dish with the milk, asparagus spears and broad (fava) beans. Cover with vented cling wrap (plastic wrap) and cook for 4 minutes, turning once, until the fish is done. Keep warm.

◆ Put the tagliatelle in a pot and pour over boiling water to just cover. Add a pinch of salt and the oil, cover and cook for 3–4 minutes, until *al dente* (firm to the bite).

◆ Pour pools of sauce onto 4 heated serving plates. Drain the noodles well and divide between the plates of sauce.

◆ Flake the haddock on top of the noodles, dust with paprika and serve with the broad (fava) beans and asparagus spears.

DABS WITH CARROTS AND CELERY

SERVES 4 / SET: FULL

Ingredients

1 bulb fennel, sliced
3 carrots, peeled and cut into strips lengthways
3 sticks (stacks) celery, sliced
45 ml/3 tbsp fish stock or milk
15 ml/1 tbsp lemon juice
4 dabs
salt and freshly ground black pepper
chopped parsley or fennel fronds
lemon wedges

◆ Put the sliced fennel, carrots and celery in a large oblong dish and add the fish stock or milk and lemon juice. Cover with vented cling wrap (plastic wrap) and cook for 8 minutes, stirring once, until the vegetables are tender.
◆ Lay the fish on top of the vegetables and cover again. Cook for 3 minutes, turning the dish once, until the fish are done.
◆ Lay the fish on warmed plates and spoon the vegetables beside them. Add a little of the cooking liquor, season and garnish with parsley or fennel fronds.
◆ Serve with lemon wedges.

FILLETS OF HALIBUT WITH RED PEPPER SAUCE

SERVES 4 / SET: FULL

Ingredients

1 courgette (zucchini), chopped
4 small tomatoes, skinned, seeded and chopped
15 ml/1 tbsp water
1 large red pepper, seeded and chopped
½ clove of garlic, crushed (minced)
a little chopped onion
2/3 cup/150 ml/¼ pt canned consommé
15 ml/1 tbsp sherry
salt and white pepper
4 fillets of halibut, about 175 g/6 oz each, skinned
a little butter
a lemon

◆ First make the garnish. Put the courgette (zucchini) and tomatoes in a dish with the water. Cook for 2 minutes. Set aside.
◆ Make the sauce. Combine the pepper, garlic, onion, consommé and sherry in a small bowl and cook for 5 minutes, until the pepper is very soft. Blend in a liquidizer, season and keep warm.
◆ Trim the halibut to 4 square shapes. Lay in a buttered dish and dot with butter. Cover with vented cling wrap (plastic wrap) and cook for 3–4 minutes, turning once, until done.
◆ Put the fish on 4 heated plates. Add a spoonful of sauce and garnish with a little mound of the courgette and tomato mixture and the lemon.

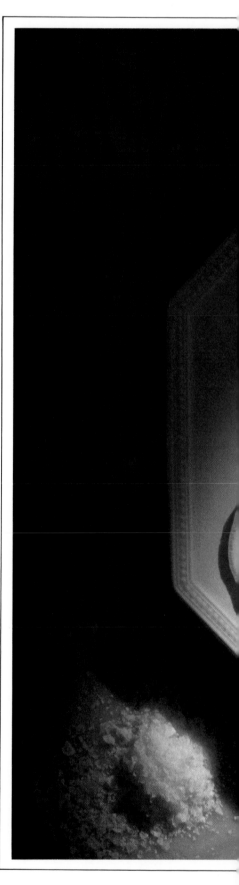

Fillets of halibut with red pepper sauce

PRAWNS (SHRIMP) AND COURGETTES (ZUCCHINI) IN TOMATO SAUCE

SERVES 4 / SET: FULL

Ingredients

15 ml/1 tbsp oil
2 shallots, chopped
4 baby courgettes (zucchini), sliced
1½ cups/400 g/14 oz tinned (canned) tomatoes, sieved (strained)
2½ cups/400 g/14 oz peeled prawns (shrimp)
freshly chopped basil
salt and freshly ground black pepper

◆ Put the oil in a bowl and cook for 30 seconds. Add the shallots and courgettes (zucchini) and cook for 3 minutes.

◆ Stir in the sieved (strained) tomatoes and the prawns (shrimp) and cook, covered with vented cling wrap, for 5 minutes, until hot through.

◆ Sprinkle with plenty of basil and season to taste with salt and pepper.

◆ Serve with rice.

SQUID WITH BEETROOT (BEETS)

S E R V E S   4 / S E T :   F U L L

Ingredients

approx. 3 cups/500 g/1 lb small squid
15 ml/1 tbsp olive oil
1 small onion, chopped
1 clove garlic, crushed (minced)
1 stalk (stack) celery, finely chopped
2 cooked beetroot (beets) chopped
½ glass dry white wine
15 ml/1 tbsp tomato purée (paste)
salt and freshly ground black pepper
celery tips

◆ First clean the squid. Remove the eyes, mouth, ink sac and outer membrane. Take out the cuttlefish bone. Wash the squid well, then slice body and tentacles.

◆ Put the olive oil in a pot and cook for 30 seconds. Stir in the onion and garlic and cook for 2 minutes.

◆ Add the celery, beetroot (beets) and squid. Mix the white wine and tomato purée (paste) and pour over the squid. Cover and cook for 8 minutes, or until the squid is tender.

◆ Season with salt and pepper and serve garnished with celery tips.

Squid with beetroot (beets)

ANCHOVY AND POTATO BAKE

SERVES 4 / SET: FULL AND MEDIUM

Ingredients

3 tbsp/40 g/1½ oz butter
1 large onion, finely sliced
8 cups/1 kg/2 lb potatoes, peeled and coarsely grated
¼ cup/50 g/2 oz canned anchovies, drained, soaked in milk for 30 minutes, then dried and chopped
30 ml/2 tbsp capers
cayenne pepper
⅔ cup/150 ml/¼ pt single (light) cream
45 ml/3 tbsp grated Parmesan cheese

◆ Put the butter in a dish and cook on full for 45 seconds. Add the onion, cover and cook on full for 3 minutes.

◆ Mix in the potatoes, cover and cook on full for 8 minutes, until soft.

◆ Stir in the anchovies and capers and season with cayenne pepper. Pour on the cream and top with grated Parmesan.

◆ Cook on medium power for 4 minutes, until hot through.

RED MULLET WITH HAM

SERVES 4 / SET: FULL AND MEDIUM

Ingredients

4 red mullet, cleaned
4 slices ham
a little butter
⅔ cup/150 ml/5 fl oz single (light) cream
7½ ml/½ tbsp tomato purée (paste)
fresh herbs to garnish
12 thin slices of courgette (zucchini), cooked for 30 seconds

◆ Lay the mullet on the ham in a greased dish. Dot with butter. Cover with vented cling wrap (plastic wrap) and cook on full power for 3–4 minutes, turning once.

◆ Mix the cream with the tomato purée (paste) in a bowl and cook for 1 minute on medium power.

◆ Spoon the sauce onto 4 heated plates. Put the ham slices in the sauce and the mullet on top. Garnish each serving with fresh herbs and 3 courgette (zucchini) slices.

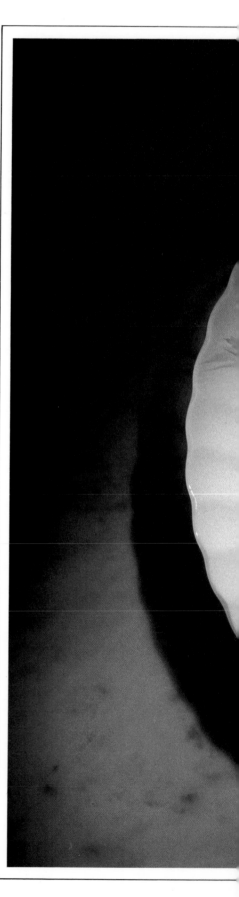

Red mullet with ham

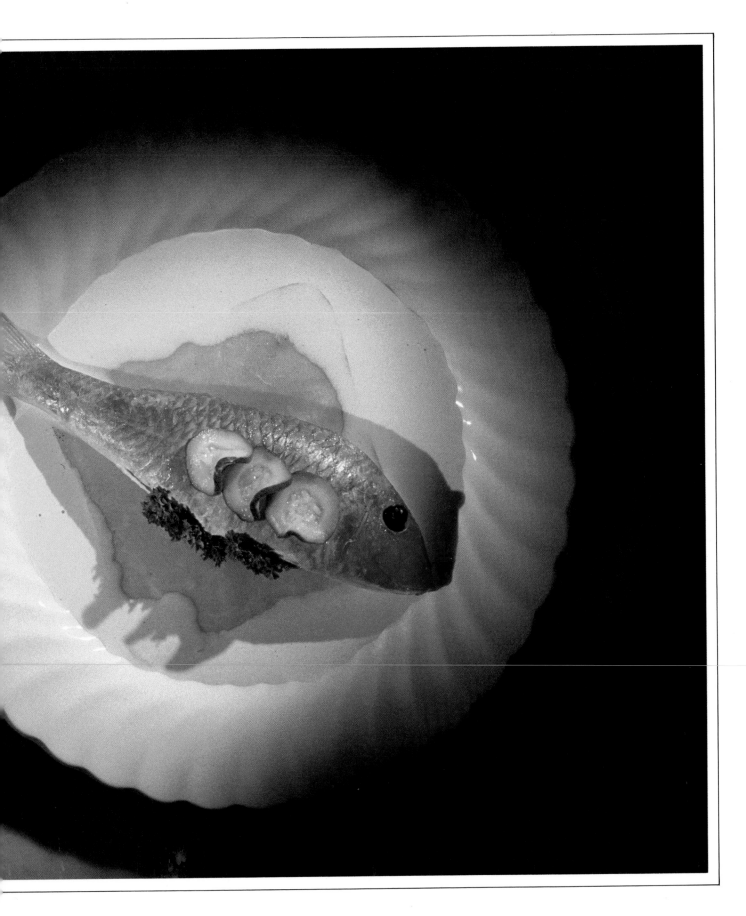

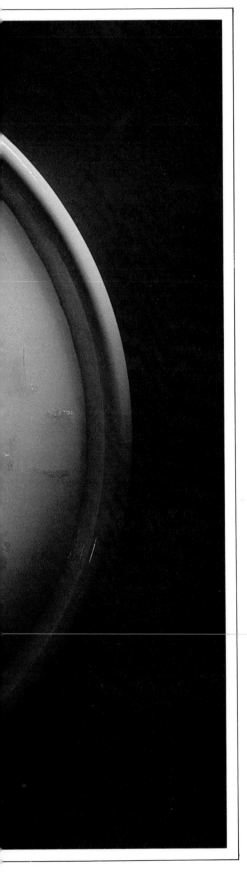

HALIBUT IN ORANGE SAUCE WITH BROCCOLI AND ALMONDS

SERVES 4 / SET: FULL

Ingredients
2 tbsp/25 g/1 oz butter
3 tbsp/25 g/1 oz cornflour (cornstarch)
1¼ cups/300 ml/½ pt orange juice
grated rind of 1 orange
4 halibut steaks, about 150 g/5 oz each
30 ml/2 tbsp water
8 spears broccoli
⅓ cup/50 g/2 oz flaked (slivered) almonds

◆ Put the butter in a bowl and cook for 1 minute. Stir in the cornflour (cornstarch) and cook for 1 minute. Stir in the orange juice and cook for 3 minutes, whisking after each minute. Stir in the orange rind. Keep the sauce warm.
◆ Put the halibut steaks in a dish with the water. Add the broccoli and the almond slivers. Cover with vented cling wrap (plastic wrap) and cook for 4 minutes, rearranging once, until the fish is done and the broccoli is tender.
◆ Pour the orange sauce over 4 heated plates, add the halibut and garnish with the broccoli and almonds.

FILLETS OF TURBOT IN CRAB SAUCE WITH RED PEPPERS

SERVES 4 / SET: FULL

Ingredients
1 red pepper, seeded and cut into julienne strips
30 ml/2 tbsp water
⅔ cup/150 ml/¼ pt single (light) cream
50 g/2 oz tinned (canned) dressed crab meat
salt and white pepper
4 turbot fillets
2 tbsp/25 g/1 oz butter

◆ Put the strips of red pepper in a dish with the water. Cover with vented cling wrap (plastic wrap) and cook for 4–5 minutes, until tender, stirring once. Set aside.
◆ Mash the cream into the crab meat until smooth. Season to taste with salt and white pepper.
◆ Put the turbot in a dish, dot with butter, cover with vented cling wrap (plastic wrap) and cook for 4 minutes, rearranging once.
◆ Cook the crab sauce for 1–2 minutes to heat through.
◆ Spoon a pool of crab sauce onto 4 heated plates, put the fish on top and garnish with strips of red pepper.

Halibut in orange sauce with broccoli and almonds

FILLETS OF SOLE WITH SPINACH SAUCE

S E R V E S   4   /   S E T :   F U L L

Ingredients

5 tbsp/65 g/2 1/2 oz butter
6 tbsp/40 g/1 1/2 oz flour
1 1/4 cups/300 ml/1/2 pt milk
1 egg yolk
1/4 cup/100 g/4 oz frozen spinach, defrosted and squeezed very thoroughly to drain
salt and freshly ground black pepper
2 soles, filleted
a squeeze of lemon juice
fine slices of carrot, cut into flower shapes
snipped chives

Serve this creamy dish with a crisp salad in a contrasting colour – radicchio would go very well.

◆ First make the sauce. Put 3 tbsp/ 40 g/1 1/2 oz of the butter in a bowl and cook for 1 minute. Stir in the flour and cook for 1 minute. Pour on the milk and cook for 3 minutes, whisking after every minute. Stir in the egg yolk and spinach and season to taste. Cook for 1 minute, then keep warm.

◆ Lay the sole fillets in a dish, dot with the remaining butter and sprinkle with lemon juice. Cook for 3–4 minutes, rearranging once.

◆ Arrange the fillets on heated plates, pour the sauce over and garnish with carrot slices and chives to look like flowers and stalks.

◆ Serve at once.

Fillets of sole with spinach sauce

SOUSED HERRING

SERVES 4 / SET: FULL

Ingredients

15 ml/1 tbsp oil

1 onion, cut into rings

1 large apple, peeled, cored and sliced

15 ml/1 tbsp pickling spices

1 bay leaf

⅔ cup/150 ml/¼ pt cider vinegar

4 herring, cleaned and boned

◆ Put the oil in a dish and cook for 30 seconds. Add the onion and cook for 2 minutes.

◆ Mix the onion with the apple, add the pickling spices and bay leaf and pour over the cider vinegar. Lay the herring on top. Cover with vented cling wrap (plastic wrap). Cook until the vinegar boils and then for about 3 more minutes, until the fish are done. Leave to cool.

◆ Serve the fish cold with a spoonful of the cooking vinegar and apple and onion slices on top.

MUSSEL SALAD

SERVES 4 / SET: FULL

Ingredients

1 tbsp/15 g/½ oz butter
1 small onion, chopped
4 cups/500 g/1 lb mussels, well scrubbed
30 ml/2 tbsp lemon juice
30 ml/2 tbsp dry white wine
4 sticks (stacks) celery, sliced
¾ cup/100 g/4 oz cooked green beans, cut into bite-size pieces
1 red pepper, cut into julienne strips
1½ cups/250 g/8 oz cooked potatoes, sliced
30 ml/2 tbsp mayonnaise
chopped parsley
salt and freshly ground black pepper

◆ Put the butter in a deep pot and cook for 30 seconds. Add the onion and cook for 2 minutes.

◆ Put in the mussels (discarding any that are broken or open), pour in the lemon juice and white wine and cook, covered, for 3–4 minutes, until the mussels have opened.

◆ Discard any closed shells. Allow the mussels to cool, then remove them from their shells.

◆ Mix the mussels in a large bowl with the celery, green beans, red pepper and potatoes. Stir the mayonnaise into the cooking liquor and onion and pour over the salad.

◆ Add chopped parsley and seasoning, mix well and serve.

KEDGEREE

SERVES 4 / SET: FULL

Ingredients

1 cup/250 g/8 oz rice
2½ cups/600 ml/1 pt boiling fish or chicken stock
salt
4 kipper fillets (kippered herrings)
30 ml/2 tbsp water
2 tbsp/25 g/1 oz butter
2–4 hardboiled (hard-cooked) eggs, chopped or sliced
cayenne pepper
2 tomatoes, sliced or cut into wedges
sprigs of parsley
a few prawns (shrimp) (optional)

A traditional breakfast dish, kedgeree makes a good evening snack and can be put together easily from the storecupboard (pantry).

◆ Put the rice in a pot and pour over the boiling stock. Season with a pinch of salt, cover and cook for 12 minutes. Remove from the oven and leave covered while you prepare the kippers (kippered herrings).

◆ Lay the kippers in a dish with the water, cover and cook for 2 minutes. Flake the kippers with a fork, discarding any bits of skin.

◆ Stir the kippers, butter and eggs into the rice and season with cayenne pepper to taste. Garnish with tomatoes, parsley and a few prawns (shrimp) if liked.

◆ Serve hot.

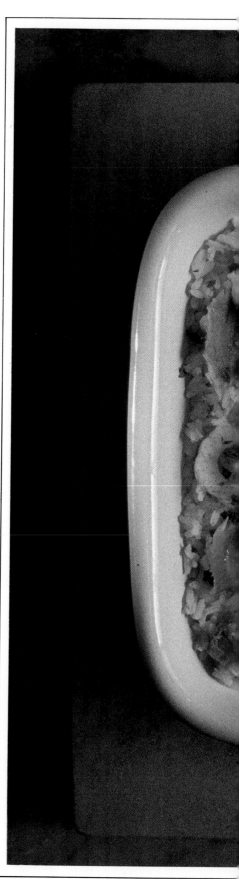

Kedgeree

KING PRAWNS (SHRIMP) WITH MALTAISE SAUCE

SERVES 4 / SET: FULL AND MEDIUM

Ingredients

½ cup/100 g/4 oz butter, diced

grated rind and juice of 1 orange

3 egg yolks

salt and white pepper

12 king prawns

curly endive

◆ Put the butter in a bowl and heat on full power for 1½ minutes until melted.

◆ Whisk the orange rind and juice with the egg yolks and whisk into the hot butter, blending well. Season to taste with salt and white pepper, then cook on medium power for 1 minute, watching to make sure that the sauce does not boil.

◆ Arrange the king prawns on curly endive on 4 plates and serve with the Maltaise sauce. Provide your guests with finger bowls and large napkins.

VARIATION This is an excellent way of serving langoustines.

King prawns (shimp) with maltaise sauce

RED SNAPPER WITH LEMON AND LIME

SERVES 4 / SET: FULL

Ingredients

2 tbsp/25 g/1 oz butter

½ fennel bulb, chopped

juice of ½ lemon

juice of 1 lime

4 red snapper, cleaned

slices of lemon

slices of lime

fronds of fennel

◆ Put the butter in a dish and cook for 30 seconds. Add the chopped fennel, cover with vented cling wrap (plastic wrap) and cook for 3 minutes, stirring once.

◆ Pour on the lemon and lime juice and lay the red snapper on top of the fennel. Cover with vented cling wrap (plastic wrap) and cook for 4 minutes, until done, turning the dish once.

◆ Arrange the fish and fennel on 4 heated plates and spoon over the juice. Garnish with slices of lemon and lime and fennel fronds.

MONKFISH, CAULIFLOWER AND MANGETOUT (SNOW) PEAS

SERVES 4 / SET: FULL

Ingredients

¹/₂ cauliflower
30 ml/2 tbsp water
2¹/₄ cups/350 g/12 oz mangetout (snow) peas
1¹/₂ cups/350 g/12 oz monkfish pieces (or other firm white fish, eg grouper)
30 ml/2 tbsp dry sherry
30 ml/2 tbsp soy sauce
1 clove garlic, crushed (minced)

This is a very popular dish in Singapore, where it is served with a bowl of rice.

◆ Break the cauliflower into florets, discarding tough stalks and leaves. Put it in a bowl with the water, cover and cook for 3–4 minutes, until you can pierce the stalks with the point of a sharp knife. Stir once during cooking.

◆ Cut the stalks from the mangetout (snow) peas. Put the cauliflower and peas in a bowl with the monkfish.

◆ Combine the sherry, soy sauce and garlic. Pour over the vegetables and monkfish, stirring well. Leave for 30 minutes to marinate, stirring occasionally.

◆ Cover the bowl with vented cling wrap (plastic wrap) and cook for 3 minutes, stirring once.

◆ Serve immediately.

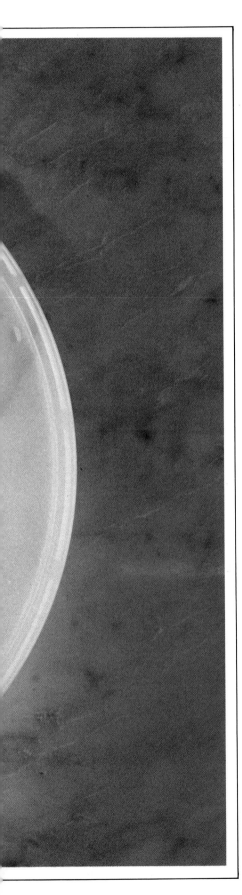

PRAWNS (SHRIMP) ST JACQUES

SERVES 4 / SET: FULL

Ingredients

3 tbsp/40 g/1½ oz butter
6 tbsp/40 g/1½ oz flour
⅔ cup/150 ml/¼ pt milk
⅔ cup/150 ml/¼ pt single (light) cream
60 ml/4 tbsp grated Parmesan cheese
salt and freshly ground black pepper
3 cups/500 g/1 lb prawns (shrimp) shelled weight
TOPPING
2 cups/500 g/1 lb cooked mashed potato
3 tbsp/40 g/1½ oz butter
salt
30 ml/2 tbsp grated Parmesan cheese
15 ml/1 tbsp golden breadcrumbs
chopped parsley

◆ Put the butter in a bowl and cook for 1½ minutes until melted. Stir in the flour and cook for 1 minute. Stir in the milk and cook for 1 minute. Stir or whisk in the cream and cook for 1 minute. Stir in the cheese and cook for 1 minute. Season the sauce to taste and whisk or stir until smooth.

◆ Reserve some prawns (shrimp) for the garnish. Stir the peeled prawns into the sauce.

◆ Mash the potato with the butter and season with salt.

◆ Divide the prawn mixture between 4 scallop shells, top with the mashed potato and sprinkle with Parmesan cheese, golden breadcrumbs and parsley. Heat through in the microwave for 1 minute, decorate with the unshelled prawns and serve hot.

MONKFISH AND BABY LEEKS IN CHEESE SAUCE

SERVES 4 / SET: FULL

Ingredients

1¾ cups/400 g/14 oz monkfish (or any other firm white fish, eg grouper), skinned and cut into pieces
8 baby leeks, washed and trimmed
30–45 ml/2–3 tbsp water
3 tbsp/40 g/1½ oz butter
6 tbsp/40 g/1½ oz flour
1¼ cups/300 ml/½ pt milk
⅓ cup/50 g/2 oz grated Parmesan cheese
salt and freshly ground black pepper

◆ Put the monkfish (or equivalent) and leeks in a large oblong dish and add the water. Cover with vented cling wrap (plastic wrap) and cook for 5 minutes, rearranging once, until the fish is done and the leeks are tender. Set aside while you make the sauce.

◆ Put the butter in a jug and cook for 45 seconds. Stir in the flour. Pour on the milk and cook for 3 minutes, whisking after each minute. Stir in the cheese and cook for a further minute. Whisk again. Season to taste.

◆ Pour the sauce over the leeks and monkfish and heat through before serving.

Prawns (shrimp) St Jacques

COD STEAKS WITH TWO SAUCES

SERVES 4 / SET: FULL AND MEDIUM

Ingredients

1 ripe avocado pear (avocado)
1¼ cups/300 ml/½ pt single (light) cream
salt and white pepper
black pepper
1⅓ cups/250 g/8 oz strawberries
a squeeze of lemon juice
4 cod steaks
30 ml/2 tbsp milk

Strawberries and avocados make a surprisingly good combination, and they look very pretty together too.

◆ First make the sauces. Cut the avocado in half with a sharp knife and remove the stone. Scoop out the flesh from one half and put in the blender with half the cream. Blend until smooth. Season with salt and white pepper and put in a jug.

◆ Hull the strawberries. Put about ¾ cup/150 g/5 oz in the blender with the remaining cream and liquidize until smooth. Season with salt and black pepper and put in a jug.

◆ Prepare the garnish. Carefully remove the other half of the avocado from its shell without spoiling the shape. Cut into slices. Sprinkle with lemon juice to stop it going brown. Slice the remaining strawberries. Set aside.

◆ Put the cod steaks in a dish, add the milk and cover with vented cling wrap (plastic wrap). Cook on full for 4 minutes, or until done, turning once.

◆ Put the jugs of sauce in the microwave and cook on medium for 1–2 minutes, until warmed through.

◆ Put the cod on 4 heated serving plates. Spoon the avocado sauce to one side of the fish and the strawberry sauce to the other.

◆ Garnish with the avocado and strawberry slices and serve at once.

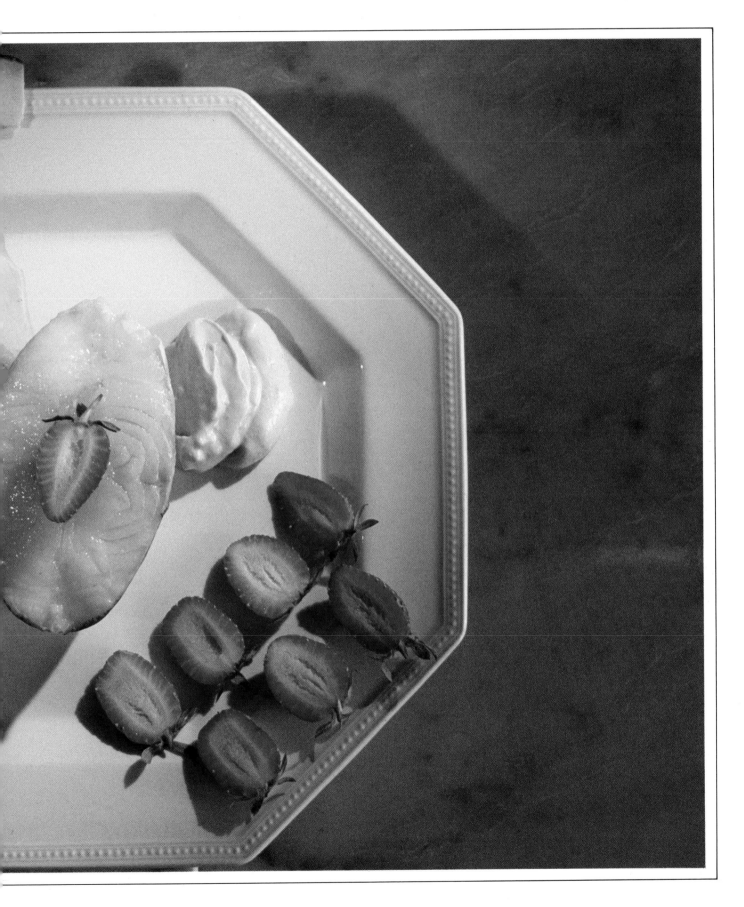

SMOKED HADDOCK AND POACHED EGG

SERVES 2 / SET: FULL AND MEDIUM

Ingredients

2 pieces smoked haddock, about 175 g/6 oz each

3 tbsp/40 g/1½ oz butter

2 tbsp milk

salt and freshly ground black pepper

2 eggs

sprigs of fennel or parsley

This is a traditional lunch dish in the East End of London, and it also makes a very good brunch or late breakfast.

◆ Put the smoked haddock in a buttered dish, dot with two-thirds of the butter and add the milk. Cover with vented cling wrap (plastic wrap) and cook on full for 3–4 minutes, turning once. Season and keep warm.

◆ Break the eggs into 2 buttered individual dishes and pierce the yolks carefully with a cocktail stick (toothpick) to prevent bursting. Cook on medium for 1½–2 minutes.

◆ Put the haddock on 2 heated plates, add the remaining butter and the poached eggs.

◆ Garnish with sprigs of fennel or parsley and serve with wholemeal (whole wheat) bread and butter.

TROUT WITH ALMONDS

SERVES 4 / SET: FULL

Ingredients

3 tbsp/40 g/1½ oz butter
⅓ cup/50 g/2 oz flaked (slivered) almonds
juice of 1 lemon
4 trout, cleaned, heads off or on, as liked
salt and freshly ground black pepper

◆ Put the butter in a large oblong dish. Cook for 1 minute. Stir in the almonds and cook for 1 minute. Stir in the lemon juice.

◆ Add the trout, turning them in the dish to coat. Cover with vented cling wrap (plastic wrap) and cook for 4 minutes, until done through, turning once.

◆ Spoon the almonds and lemon butter over the fish to serve.

TROUT STUFFED WITH WATERCRESS

SERVES 4 / SET: FULL

Ingredients

4 small trout
1 tbsp/15 g/½ oz butter
1 clove garlic, crushed (minced)
1 bunch watercress, trimmed and chopped
4 tbsp breadcrumbs
1 egg, beaten
salt and freshly ground black pepper

◆ First make the stuffing. Put the butter in a bowl and cook for 30 seconds. Add the garlic and cook for 1 minute.

◆ Mix together the watercress, breadcrumbs, garlic butter and beaten egg. Season to taste and stuff the trout with this mixture.

◆ Lay the trout in a dish and cover with vented cling wrap (plastic wrap). Cook for 4 minutes, rearranging once, until done.

◆ Serve with mashed potatoes and a tomato salad.

HERRINGS WITH HORSERADISH SAUCE

SERVES 4 / SET: FULL

Ingredients

3 egg yolks
45 ml/3 tbsp white wine vinegar
6 tbsp/75 g/3 oz butter, diced
6 tbsp/40 g/1½ oz grated horseradish
salt and freshly ground white pepper
4 herrings, whole or filleted

◆ Whisk the egg yolks with the wine vinegar. Put the butter in a bowl and cook for 1½ minutes until melted. Whisk the yolks and vinegar into the butter. Cook for 30 seconds.

◆ Whisk again, adding the horseradish gradually. Whisk until cool and thick. Season with salt and white pepper. Set aside.

◆ Put the herrings in a dish, cover with vented cling wrap (plastic wrap) and cook for 3–4 minutes, until done, turning once.

◆ Arrange the herrings on 4 heated plates and serve with green beans if liked and the horseradish sauce.

Herrings with horseradish sauce

CRISPY WHITING FILLETS

S E R V E S 4 / S E T : F U L L

Ingredients
8 whiting fillets
salt and freshly ground black pepper
2 eggs, beaten
golden breadcrumbs
15 ml/1 tbsp oil
2 tbsp/25 g/1 oz butter
lemon slices

◆ Sprinkle the whiting with salt and pepper. Dip in beaten egg and then in golden breadcrumbs, pressing them on well to cover the fish.

◆ Heat a browning dish to maximum, according to the manufacturer's instructions. Add the oil and butter. Cook for 30 seconds. Protecting your hands with oven gloves, tilt the dish so that it is well oiled.

◆ Lay the whiting fillets in the dish (cook them in 2 batches if necessary) and cook for 4 minutes, turning once.

◆ Serve with lemon slices and wholemeal (whole wheat) bread and butter and a salad if liked.

Crispy whiting fillets

CELERIAC, WALNUT AND PRAWN (SHRIMP) SALAD

S E R V E S 4 / S E T : F U L L

Ingredients
1 celeriac
45 ml/3 tbsp water
15 ml/1 tbsp lemon juice
⅓ cup/50 g/2 oz walnut pieces
2½ cups/400 g/14 oz prawns (shrimp), peeled (leave some unpeeled for garnish)
⅔ cup/150 ml/¼ pt yogurt
15 ml/1 tbsp tinned (canned) dressed crab meat
salt and white pepper

This makes an excellent and unusual starter. If you have to leave the celeriac between preparing and cooking it, put it in a bowl of cold water acidulated with lemon juice and store in the fridge.

◆ Peel the celeriac and cut into julienne strips. Put it in a dish with the water and lemon juice, cover with vented cling wrap (plastic wrap) and cook for about 4 minutes, until the celeriac is cooked but still crisp, shaking or stirring once.

◆ Drain the celeriac and rinse it under cold running water. Mix it with the walnuts and prawns (shrimp).

◆ Mix together the yogurt and crab meat to make a delicate pink seafood sauce. Season with salt and white pepper.

◆ Serve the salad in pools of the pink sauce, garnished with the unpeeled prawns (shrimp).

FILLETS OF TURBOT IN BEETROOT (BEET) SAUCE

*S E R V E S   4 / S E T :   D E F R O S T
A N D   F U L L*

Ingredients

1 beetroot (beet), cooked

⅔ cup/150 ml/5 fl oz single (light) cream

salt and white pepper

4 turbot fillets, about 175 g/6 oz each, skinned

a little butter

spring onion (scallion) tassels

Spring onion (scallion) tassels are made by cutting 2 slits through the top of each trimmed and washed onion, at right angles to one another, and leaving them in ice water until the tops curl back.

◆ Peel and chop the beetroot (beet). Put it in the liquidizer with the cream and reduce to a smooth sauce. Season to taste with salt and pepper. Cook for 1–2 minutes on defrost to heat through. Keep warm.

◆ Trim the fillets to even size squares, lay in a buttered dish and dot with butter. Cover with vented cling wrap (plastic wrap) and cook for 3–4 minutes, turning once, until cooked through.

◆ Spoon the sauce onto 4 heated plates, lay the fish on top and garnish with spring onion (scallion) tassels.

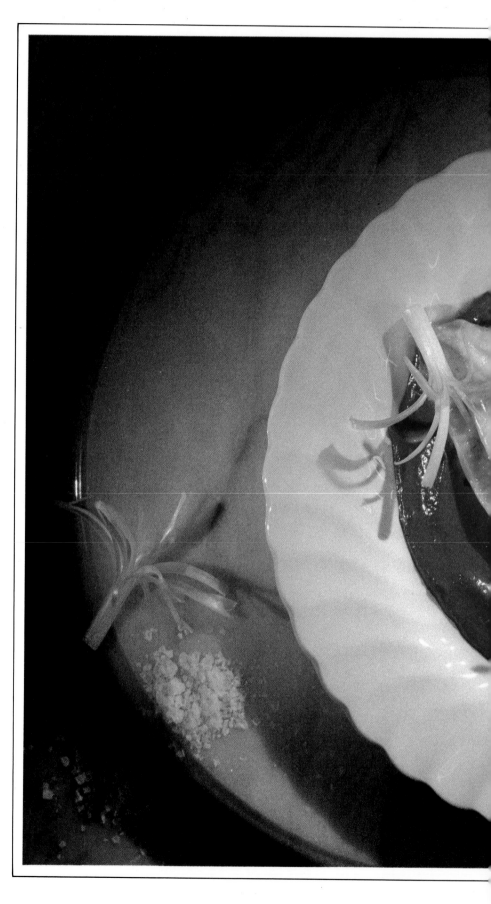

Fillets of turbot in beetroot (beet) sauce

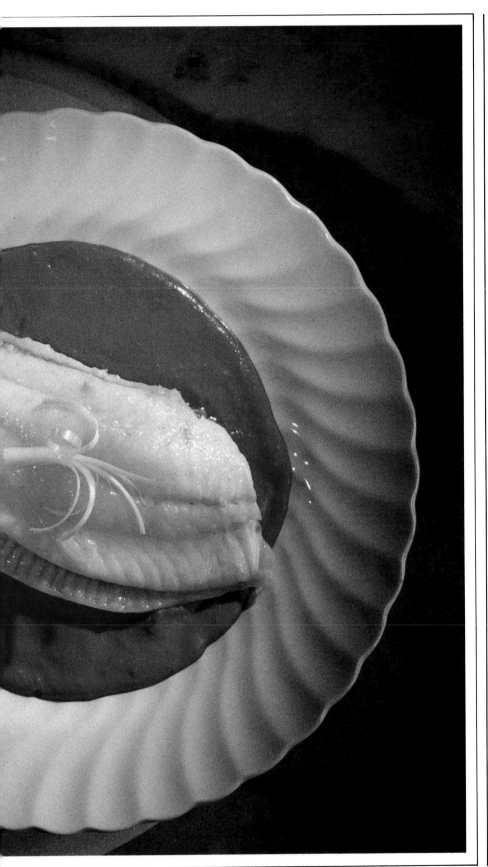

FISH KORMA

*SERVES 4 / SET: FULL
AND MEDIUM*

Ingredients

3 cups/750 g/1½ lb cod, skinned and cubed

⅔ cup/150 ml/¼ pt yogurt

5 ml/1 tsp turmeric

1 clove garlic, crushed (minced)

3 tbsp/40 g/1½ oz butter

1 large onion, finely sliced

5 cardamoms

3 cloves

◆ Put the fish in a dish. Mix together the yogurt, turmeric and garlic and stir into the fish. Leave to marinate for an hour.

◆ Put the butter in a large dish and cook on full power for 45 seconds. Add the onions and spices, cover and cook on full power for 3 minutes.

◆ Stir in the fish and marinade, cover and cook on medium power for 10 minutes, stirring once.

◆ Serve with rice.

EELS WITH PEAS AND PARSLEY SAUCE

SERVES 4 / SET: FULL

Ingredients

3 cups/750 g/1½ lb eels, skinned, boned and cut into 5-cm/2-in pieces (try to buy it ready prepared)
⅔ cup/150 ml/¼ pt boiling fish stock (or see method)
2 slivers of lemon
3 tbsp/40 g/1½ oz butter
6 tbsp/40 g/1½ oz flour
⅔ cup/150 ml/¼ pt milk
salt and freshly ground black pepper
30 ml/2 tbsp chopped parsley
1¾ cups/200 g/7 oz tinned (canned) marrowfat (large) peas, drained

◆ Put the eels in a deep oblong dish and add the boiling fish stock. Alternatively, use the liquor from the tinned (canned) peas. Add the lemon slivers, cover with vented cling wrap and cook for 5 minutes, until tender. Discard the lemon.

◆ Put the butter in a jug and cook for 45 seconds. Stir in the flour. Pour on the milk and the cooking liquor from the eels and cook for 3 minutes, whisking after each minute. Season and stir in the parsley.

◆ Add the peas to the dish of eels and pour over the sauce. Reheat for 1 minute, then serve with mashed potatoes.

MULLET WITH TOMATOES AND BASIL

SERVES 4 / SET: FULL

Ingredients

15 ml/1 tbsp olive oil
15 ml/1 tbsp chopped onion
1 clove garlic, crushed (minced)
1¼ cups/350 g/12 oz ripe tomatoes, peeled, seeded and chopped
a few leaves of basil or 5 ml/1 tsp dried basil
4 red mullet, about 175 g/6 oz each, scaled and gutted
a little butter
30 ml/2 tbsp tinned (canned) peas, drained
30 ml/2 tbsp tinned (canned) yellow or white beans, drained

◆ First make the sauce. Put the oil in a bowl and cook for 30 seconds. Stir in the onion and garlic and cook for 2 minutes. Stir in the tomatoes and basil, cover and cook for 4 minutes, or until soft, stirring twice.

◆ Put the mullet in a buttered dish, cover with vented cling wrap (plastic wrap) and cook for 4 minutes, until done, turning once.

◆ Put the peas and beans in a bowl and cook for 1 minute.

◆ Put a portion of mixed peas and beans onto 4 heated plates, lay the mullet on top and pour the sauce over.

Mullet with tomatoes and basil

SPICY FISH CASSEROLE WITH RICE

S E R V E S   4   /   S E T :   F U L L

Ingredients

approx. 3 cups/750 g/1½ lb cod fillets, skinned and cut into chunks

salt and freshly ground black pepper

15 ml/1 tbsp turmeric (approx.)

30 ml/2 tbsp olive oil

1 large onion, finely sliced

2 cloves garlic, crushed (minced)

1 green pepper, cut into julienne strips

1 red pepper, cut into julienne strips

1 cup/250 g/8 oz long-grain rice

1½ cups/400 g/14 oz tinned (canned) tomatoes, drained and juice reserved

boiling water or fish stock

◆ Sprinkle the cod with salt and dust with turmeric. Set aside.

◆ Put the olive oil into a large pot and cook for 30 seconds. Add the onion, garlic and peppers. Cover and cook for 3 minutes.

◆ Stir in the rice. Make the reserved tomato juice up to 2½ cups/600 ml/ 1 pt with boiling water or fish stock, pour over the rice, cover and cook for 8 minutes.

◆ Stir in the drained tomatoes and the cod. Cover and cook for 4–6 minutes, until the fish and rice are done.

◆ Let the pot stand for 5 minutes, check the seasoning and serve.

SOLE WITH SAGE AND BUTTER

SERVES 2 / SET: FULL

Ingredients

2 whole sole, skinned, each weighing
250–300 g/8–10 oz
8 sage leaves
2 tbsp/25 g/1 oz butter, diced
salt and freshly ground black pepper
lemon wedges

◆ Lay the soles in a dish with the sage leaves and dot with butter. Cover with vented cling wrap (plastic wrap) and cook for about 3 minutes, turning the dish once. As sole is so delicate, it is better to undercook and add on a few seconds if it is still not done.

◆ When the fish is ready, transfer to heated plates, season with salt and pepper and serve with lemon wedges.

FILLETS OF COD IN MUSTARD SAUCE

SERVES 4 / SET: FULL AND DEFROST

Ingredients

diamonds of red and green pepper
15 ml/1 tbsp water
4 cod fillets, weighing about 175 g/6 oz each
a squeeze of lemon juice
2/3 cup/150 ml/5 fl oz single (light) cream
5 ml/1 tsp English mustard powder

◆ First make the garnish. Cut out the pepper diamonds and put them in a dish with the water. Cook, covered with vented cling wrap (plastic wrap), on full for 2 minutes.

◆ Trim the cod fillets so that they are of even size and square in shape. Lay them in a dish, sprinkle with lemon juice and cover with vented cling wrap (plastic wrap). Cook on full for 4 minutes, turning once, until cooked.

◆ Mix the cream with the mustard powder to give it a delicate yellow hue and a pleasantly pungent taste. Heat through on defrost power for 1–2 minutes.

◆ Pour a pool of sauce onto each of 4 heated plates.

◆ Lay the cod fillets on the sauce and garnish with the pepper shapes.

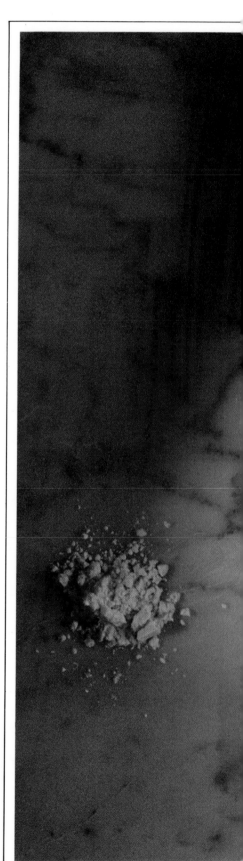

Fillets of cod in mustard sauce

CHINESE PRAWNS (SHRIMP) WITH VEGETABLES

SERVES 4 / SET: FULL

Ingredients

500 g/1 lb unpeeled prawns (shrimp)

45 ml/3 tbsp soy sauce

15 ml/1 tbsp sherry

1 clove garlic, crushed (minced)

15 ml/1 tbsp chopped onion

1 scant cup/200 g/7 oz tinned (canned) water chestnuts, drained

2 cups/200 g/7 oz button mushrooms

1 cup/200 g/7 oz tinned (canned) baby sweetcorn (corn), drained

3/4 cup/100 g/4 oz tinned (canned) green beans, drained

1 1/2 cups/100 g/4 oz bean sprouts

strips of red and yellow pepper

Serve this dish with rice. The prawns (shrimp) look much nicer unpeeled, but peel them if you wish.

◆ Slit the prawns (shrimp) down the back and remove the blackish veins. Put them in a bowl and stir in the soy sauce, sherry, garlic and onion. Leave to marinate for an hour, stirring occasionally.

◆ Stir in the remaining ingredients, cover with vented cling wrap (plastic wrap) and cook for 3–4 minutes, stirring once.

◆ Garnish with pepper strips and serve hot with rice.

Chinese prawns (shrimp) with vegetables

SQUID IN TOMATO AND WINE SAUCE

SERVES 4 / SET: FULL

Ingredients

4 small squid

15 ml/1 tbsp olive oil

2 shallots, chopped

1 clove garlic, chopped

1 1/2 cups/400 g/14 oz tinned (canned) tomatoes, drained and sieved (strained)

1 glass dry white wine

chopped fresh herbs (thyme, parsley and basil)

salt and freshly ground black pepper

◆ Clean the squid. Cut away the eyes and mouth and discard, together with the ink sac and the "nib". Wash the squid thoroughly and pull off the outer membrane. Cut the body and tentacles into rings.

◆ Put the oil in a dish and cook for 30 seconds. Add the shallots and garlic and cook for 2 minutes.

◆ Stir in the sieved (strained) tomatoes, wine and squid. Sprinkle on the herbs. Cover with vented cling wrap (plastic wrap) and cook for 6–8 minutes, until the squid is tender. Season to taste with salt and pepper.

◆ Serve with rice.

FRESH VEGETABLES/COOKING GUIDE

vegetables	quantity	minutes on full
globe artichokes	4	10 – 20
asparagus spears	1½ cups/225 g/8 oz	6 – 7
aubergines (eggplant), diced	2 cups/450 g/1 lb	5 – 6
beans, broad (fava, lima), French (green) or runner	2½ cups/450 g/1 lb	8 – 10
beetroot (beets), sliced	4 cups/450 g/1 lb	7 – 8
broccoli florets	6 cups/450 g/1 lb	4 – 5
Brussels sprouts	6 cups/450 g/1 lb	8 – 10
cabbage, shredded	6 cups/450 g/1 lb	7 – 10
carrots, sliced	2 cups/225 g/8 oz	7 – 10
cauliflower florets	6 cups/450 g/1 lb	10 – 11
celery	1 head	10 – 13
corn on the cob	1	3 – 5
courgettes (zucchini), sliced	4	7 – 10
Kohlraki	4 cups/450 g/1 lb	7 – 8
leeks, sliced	4 cups/450 g/1 lb	7 – 10
marrow (squash), sliced	4 cups/450 g/1 lb	8 – 10
mushrooms, whole	2½ cups/225 g/8 oz	5 – 6
okra	4 cups/450 g/1 lb	8 – 10
onions, sliced	2 cups/225 g/8 oz	5 – 7
parsnips, sliced	2 cups/225 g/8 oz	8 – 10
peas	4 cups/450 g/1 lb	7
potatoes, new	6 cups/450 g/1 lb	8 – 10
potatoes, jacket (baked)	2 large	8
potatoes, boiled	4 cups/450 g/1 lb	6 – 7
spinach	2 cups/450 g/1 lb	5
greens, chopped	6 cups/450 g/1 lb	7 – 9
swedes (rutabaga), sliced	3 cups/450 g/1 lb	6 – 7
tomatoes, sliced	1½ cups/450 g/1 lb	2 – 3
turnips, sliced	1½ cups/225 g/8 oz	6 – 7

FROZEN VEGETABLES/COOKING GUIDE

vegetables	quantity	minutes on full
asparagus spears	1½ cups/225 g/8 oz	6 – 7
beans, broad (fava), French (green) or runner	1½ cups/225 g/8 oz	7
broccoli spears	4 cups/225 g/8 oz	6 – 8
cabbage, chopped	3 cups/225 g/8 oz	6 – 7
carrots, sliced	2 cups/225 g/8 oz	6 – 7
cauliflower florets	4 cups/225 g/8 oz	4 – 6
sweetcorn (corn)	2 cups/225 g/8 oz	4 – 6
corn on the cob	1	4 – 5
courgettes (zucchini), sliced	2 cups/225 g/8 oz	4
peas	2 cups/225 g/8 oz	4
spinach, chopped	3 cups/225 g/8 oz	5
swedes (rutabaga), cubed	2 cups/225 g/8 oz	7
turnips, sliced	1½ cups/225 g/8 oz	8
vegetables, mixed	2 cups/225 g/8 oz	4 – 6

FRESH MEAT COOKING GUIDE

meat	minutes on full per 450 g/1 lb	standing minutes
bacon (ham) roast	12 – 14	10
bacon, rashers (slices) 4	4½	—
beef, boned roasts, rare	5 – 6	15 – 20
beef, boneless roast, medium	7 – 8	15 – 20
beef, boneless roast, well-done	8 – 9	15 – 20
beef, roasts with bone, rare	5 – 6	15 – 20
beef, roasts with bone, medium	6 – 7	15 – 20
beef, roasts with bone, well-done	8 – 9	15 – 20
beef, ground, 4 patties	10	5
chicken, whole roast	8 – 10	10 – 15
chicken, portions	6 – 8	10
lamb, boned roast	7 – 8	20
lamb, boned and rolled roast	9	20
lamb, roast with bone	6 – 7	20
lamb, crown roast	9 – 10	20
lamb chops	2	10
liver, ox (beef)	8	5
liver, lamb, calves'	7	5
pork, boned rolled roast	8 – 10	15
pork, roast with bone	8 – 9	15
poussin (Cornish rock hen), pigeon, pheasant, quail	5 – 7	5
sausages (links), 4	4	—
portions	15	10
turkey, whole roast	11	10 – 15

FROZEN MEAT DEFROSTING GUIDE

meat	minutes on low per 450 g/1 lb	standing minutes
beef, boned roasts	8 – 10	30
beef, roasts on bone	8 – 10	30
beef, minced (ground)	8 – 10	2
beef steak, cubed	6 – 8	5
hamburgers, two	2	2
hamburgers, four	4	2
chicken, whole	6 – 8	30
chicken portions	5	30
duck and duckling	5 – 7	30
kidney	6 – 9	5
lamb, boned roasts	5 – 6	30 – 45
lamb, with bone	8 – 10	30 – 45
lamb chops	8 – 10	15
liver	8 – 10	5
pork, boned roasts	7 – 8	30
pork roast with bone	7 – 8	45
poussin (Cornish rock hen), grouse, pigeon, pheasant	5 – 7	10
sausages (links)	5 – 6	5
turkey, whole	10 – 12	60
veal, boned rolled roast	5 – 6	30
veal, with bone	8 – 10	45
veal chops	8 – 10	30
veal, minced (ground)	8 – 10	5

FISH
Defrost and Cooking Guide

fish	weight	defrost minutes	standing minutes	cooking in minutes on full
bass	225 g/8 oz	5 – 6	15	5 – 6
bonito tuna steaks,	225 g/8 oz	10	15	—
bream, sea-bream	225 g/8 oz	—	15	10 – 12
cod fillets	225 g/8 oz	4 – 5	5	4 – 6
cod steaks	225 g/8 oz	5	5	6
crab claws	100 g/4 oz	5	5	2 – 3
crab, dressed (crab cakes)	100 g/4 oz	2	10	—
haddock fillets	100 g/4 oz	4 – 5	5	5 – 7
haddock steaks	100 g/4 oz	4 – 5	5	4 – 7
halibut steaks	100 g/4 oz	4 – 5	5	4 – 5
hake steaks	100 g/4 oz	4 – 5	5	4 – 6
kipper (kippered herrings)	100 g/4 oz	—	—	1 – 2
kipper (kippered herrings) fillets (boil-in-the-bag)	200 g/7 oz	3	5	3
mackerel	225 g/8 oz	6 – 8	8 – 10	4 – 5
mahi-mahi	225 g/8 oz	6 – 8	—	4 – 6
red and grey mullet	225 g/8 oz	6 – 8	8 – 10	4 – 6
mussels	225 g/8 oz	5	5	—
plaice (flounder) fillets	225 g/8 oz	4 – 5	5	4
prawns (small shrimp), cooked	225 g/8 oz	5	5	—
red salmon steaks	225 g/8 oz	5	5	4 – 5
scrod fillets	225 g/8 oz	4 – 5	30	4 – 5
scampi (king prawns), raw		5	5	4 – 6
scallops	225 g/8 oz	5	5	5 – 7
snapper	225 g/8 oz	6 – 8	8 – 10	5 – 7
sole	225 g/8 oz	5 – 6	8 – 10	4
trout	225 g/8 oz	6 – 8	8 – 10	7
yellowtail	225 g/8 oz	6 – 8	8 – 10	7

TIME AND SETTINGS FOR PASTA AND GRAINS

Although there are no real time savings in cooking rice and pasta in the microwave, it may be a more foolproof way of cooking as there is no risk of sticking to the pan. Standing is usually necessary to complete cooking.

Cooking times will vary according to the type of pasta. Fresh pasta needs microwaving for only 1 minute. It requires no standing time, but should just be drained and served immediately. Times for dried pasta and rice are given below.

PASTA AND GRAINS COOKING GUIDE PER 225 G/8 OZ

food	boiling salted water to add	cooking in minutes on full	standing minutes
long grain rice (1 generous cup)	3 cups/725 ml/1¼ pt	14	5
pudding (Carolina) rice (1 generous cup)	2½ cups/600 ml/1 pt		
American (converted) rice (2½ cups)	2½ cups/600 ml/ 1 pint	12	5
brown rice	3½ cups/900 ml/ 1½ pt	30	5
egg noodles & tagliatelle (fettucini) (6 cups)	4 cups/1 litre/1¾ pt with 2 tsp oil	6 – 8	2 – 3
spaghetti	4 cups/1 litre/1¾ pt with 2 tsp oil	12	5 – 10
pasta shells (2 cups) & shapes	4 cups/1 litre/1¾ pt with 2 tsp oil	12 – 14	5 – 10
macaroni (2 cups)	4 cups/1 litre/1¾ pt with 2 tsp oil	12 – 15	2 – 3
lasagne (6 cups)	4 cups/1 litre/1¾ pt with 2 tsp oil	9	2

CAKES, BREAD AND DESSERTS DEFROSTING GUIDE

product	quantity	minutes on low	standing minutes
bread, whole loaf	1 large	6 – 8	5 – 15
bread, whole loaf	1 small	4 – 6	10
bread, sliced loaf	1 large	6 – 8	10
bread, sliced loaf	1 small	4 – 6	5
bread slice	25 g/1 oz	10 – 15 secs	1 – 2
bread rolls, crumpets,	2	15 – 20 secs	1 – 2
scones (biscuits), etc	4	25 – 35	1 – 2
cakes, cream	2	45 – 60	10
	4	1¼	10
cakes, small	2	30 – 60	5
cupcakes	4	1¼ – 1¾	5
cakes, large:			
sponge (yellow) cake	450 g/1 lb	4	10
cheesecake	23 cm/9 in	3 – 4	20
dough, pizza and bread	450 g/1 lb	4	10
dough, shortcrust and puff	227 g/8 oz	4	20
dough, shortcrust and puff	397 g/14 oz	6	20
mousse (soufflé), small	1	30 secs	15
pie, fruit or cream	650 g/26 oz	5	10
trifle	1	1	15